Exclusive Distributors:
Music Sales Limited
8/9 Frith Street, London W1V 5TZ, England.
Music Sales Pty Limited
120 Rothschild Avenue, Rosebery, NSW 2018, Australia.

Order No.AM954624
ISBN 0-7119-7290-7
This book © Copyright 1998 by Wise Publications.
Visit the Internet Music Shop at
http://www.musicsales.co.uk

Music arranged by Derek Jones.
Music processed by Paul Ewers Music Design.

Printed in the United Kingdom by Printwise (Haverhill) Limited, Suffolk.

Your Guarantee of Quality:
As publishers, we strive to produce every book to the highest commercial standards.
The music has been freshly engraved and, whilst endeavouring to retain the
original running order of the recorded album, the book has been carefully designed
to minimise awkward page turns and to make playing from it a real pleasure.
Particular care has been given to specifying acid-free, neutral-sized
paper made from pulps which have not been elemental chlorine bleached.
This pulp is from farmed sustainable forests and was
produced with special regard for the environment.
Throughout, the printing and binding have been planned to ensure
a sturdy, attractive publication which should give years of enjoyment.
If your copy fails to meet our high standards, please inform us and
we will gladly replace it.

Music Sales' complete catalogue describes thousands of titles and
is available in full colour sections by subject, direct from Music Sales Limited.
Please state your areas of interest and send a cheque/postal order
for £1.50 for postage to:
Music Sales Limited, Newmarket Road, Bury St. Edmunds, Suffolk IP33 3YB.

Wise Publications
London/New York/Sydney/Paris/Copenhagen/Madrid

CLAIRE

LISA

LEE

FAYE

STEPTRO

Music by Mike Stock & Pete Waterman
Words by Sarah Dallin & Keren Woodward

LAST THING ON MY MIND

Music by Mike Stock & Pete Waterman
Words by Sarah Dallin & Keren Woodward

1. 3. There was some - thing in — your — voice — that was tell-
(Verse 2 see block lyric)

Of all the things I was ev - er plan -
- ning for. This was the last
thing on my mind.

Verse 2:
When I looked into your eyes
There was something you weren't telling me
But in my confusion I just couldn't see
If there was any doubt
I thought that we would work it out.

But now you're *etc.*

ONE FOR SORROW

Words & Music by Mark Topham, Karl Twigg & Lance Ellington

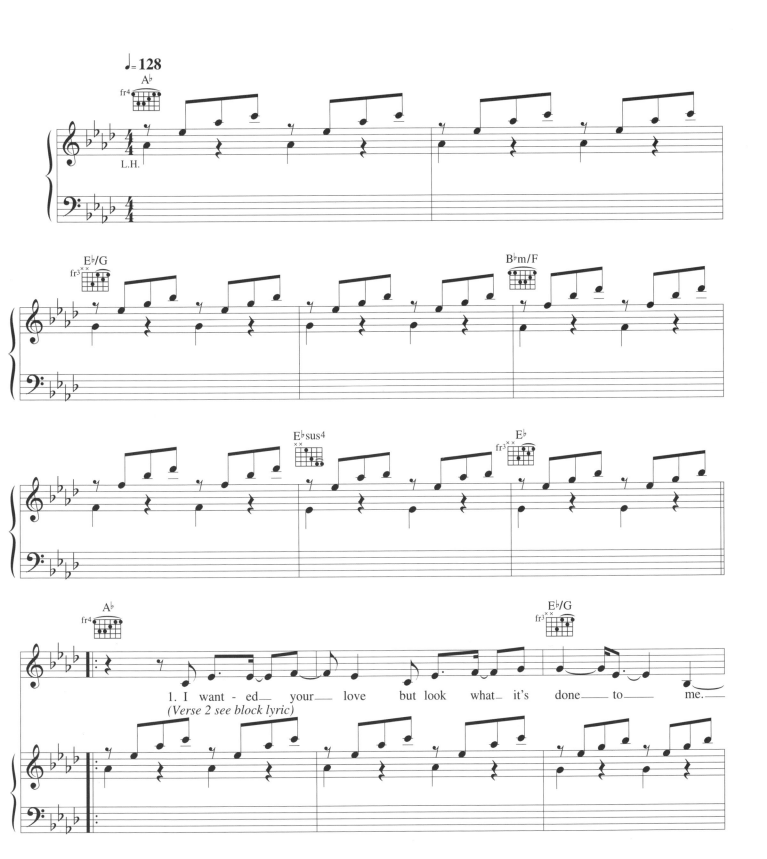

1. I want-ed your love but look what it's done to me.
(Verse 2 see block lyric)

too, ___ too ___ bad. Are you break - ing some - one els -

- es ___ heart? ___ 'Cos you're tak - ing my ___ love where ___ you are. ___ Well, I'm

one ___ for sor - row ain't it too, ___ too ___ bad a - bout ___

us?

love?

Verse 2:
I wanted your love but I got uncertainty
I tried so hard to understand you
All the good it did me
Now the places that we knew remind me of how we were
Everything is just the same
But all I feel is hurt
And do you ever think of me and how we used to be?

Oh, I know you're somewhere else *etc.*

17

5,6,7,8

Words & Music by Barry Upton & Stephen Crosby

Lyrics: It's time to be-gin now count it in... five, six, se-ven, eight. My boot scoot-in' ba-by is driv-in' me cra-zy. My ob-ses-sion from a west-ern, my dance floor date. My

ro-de-o— ro-me-o, a cow-boy god from head to toe. Wan-na make you mine, bet-ta get in line.

Five six se-ven eight.

To Coda ⊕

My

Drums

19

boot scoot-in' ba - by is driv - in' me cra - zy. My ob - ses - sion from a west - ern, my
(2° see block lyric)

dance floor date. My ro - de - o ro - me - o, a cow-boy god from head to toe. Wan - na

make you mine, bet - ta get in line. Five, six, se - ven, eight.

Foot kick-in', fin-ger click-in', lea-ther slap-ping, hand clap-pin', hip bump-in', mu-sic thump-in',

knee hitch-in', heel and toe, floor scuff-in', leg shuff-lin', big grin-nin', bo-dy spin-ning,

romp - in' stomp - in', pump - in', jump - in', slid - in', glid - in', here we go. My

Yeah!

You're mine all mine now bubba

D.%. al Coda

Gon-na rope you in, so count me in. Five, six, se - ven, eight. My

boot scoot-in' ba-by is driv-in' me cra-zy. My ob-ses-sion from a west-ern, my

dance floor date. My ro-de-o ro-me-o, a cow-boy god from head to toe. Wan-na

1. **2.**

make you mine, bet-ta get in line. Five, six, se-ven, eight. My Five, six, se-ven, eight.

2º
Tush pushin', thunder footin', cowgirl twistin', no resistin'
Drums bangin', steel twangin', two steppin', end to end
Hardwood crawlin', some four wallin', rug cuttin', cowboy struttin'
Burnin', yearnin', winding, grinding, let's begin the dance again.

HEARTBEAT

Words & Music by Jackie James

once a-gain, if your arms would on-ly let me in you'd see the

mess I'm in. I have dreamed

your heart will come and res - cue me, oh ba - by

set me free. On-ly your love can win.

Verse 2:
Here I am, my heart in the palm of your hand
Your every wish is my command
Darling understand
If I live a lie
Then all my dreams are doomed to die
Oh baby just let me try
To have my heart's desire.

You are only a heartbeat away *etc.*

THIS HEART WILL LOVE AGAIN

Words & Music by Andrew Frampton & Pete Waterman

29

Verse 2:

I know we can't go on livin' yesterdays
Wish there was something more that I could say
To make my heart forget
But now if you really have to go
Then I must somehow find the strength to show
No sadness, no regret
You won't be here tomorrow
But I'll get thru the sorrow baby.

(Now that you're gone) *etc.*

EXPERIENCED

Words & Music by Mike Stock & Pete Waterman

looked at me smil - ing, breath-ing and sigh - ing and I felt like cry - ing. She said,

"Boy can't you stay with me through the night?" You know I loved that wo - man out - ta sight.

Ev - 'ry-bo - dy needs some - one to show them how. Ev - en though her touch is just a

mem - 'ry now, I won't for - get that mo - ment I lost my in - no - cence,

the day I be-came ___ ex - pe - ri - enced. ___

2.

(Hea - ven don't.) 2. Hea - ven don't make ___ I won't for - get ___ that mo - ment

I lost my in - no - cence, the day I be - came ___ ex - pe - ri - enced. ___

Ev - 'ry - bo - dy needs ___ some - one to show them how, ___

Verse 2:
Heaven don't make mistakes
A lesson is all it takes
From the beginning
She did the teaching
And I was so willing
Sharing the feelings
Of love that way
I'm never gonna forget the day.

Everybody needs *etc.*

TOO WEAK TO RESIST

Words & Music by Dan Frampton & Pete Waterman

♩=76

1. We stood be-fore our friends and pledged e-ter-nal
(Verse 2 see block lyric)

love to have— and— to— hold. We both meant ev-'ry word and spoke of one— a-

-bove,_____ love could— not— grow cold._____ Then I

39

Verse 2:

If only I had known I'd cause you so much pain
I would not have strayed
And tho' I promise you I'll never fall again baby
I must lie in this bed that I've made
And tho' I'm hurtin' you
I swear it was the last thing on my mind
But I found myself on my own
One too many times darling.

Time can be a healer *etc.*

BETTER BEST FORGOTTEN

Words & Music by Dan Frampton & Pete Waterman

go 'cause ba - by you know___ some things are bet - ter best for - got -

- ten.___ Whoa.___

- ten. Whoa.___

Verse 2:
And baby we can't pretend
In time the scars will mend
Please believe me there's a chance
Let's take it, let's take it
And maybe at last we'll find
That love should be true not blind
You can't deceive a heart that's open wide
And even now it's not too late
To change the story's end.

So baby let's take a chance *etc.*

BACK TO YOU

Words & Music by Mark Topham & Karl Twigg

Whoa_____ back____ to you.____

C   G/B   Gm⁶/B♭

1. I know I hurt you ba - by and I'm sor - ry   but I'm back now so
(Verse 2 see block lyric)

A⁷sus⁴   A⁷/C♯   Dm⁷

don't you wor - ry.   Dar - ling what can I say,—

Gsus⁴   G

I could - n't keep my - self a - way.____

Time will an-swer all our ques-tions. All I need is your af-fec-tion.

Verse 2:

The things we said – well I guess we didn't mean them

Now I've had time I understand your reasons

Darling you won't regret, believe me I won't forget

'Cause this time our love will be much sweeter

And I promise to look a little deeper

Darling what's done is done

Our best is yet to come

Time will answer all our questions

All I need is your affection.

Wherever I go *etc.*

LOVE U MORE

Words & Music by Lucia Holm & Alan Carnell

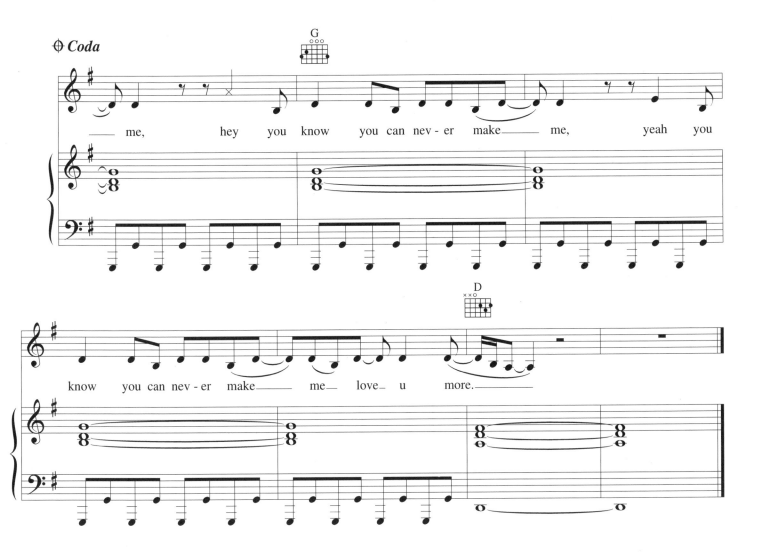

Verse 2:
You can make dew into diamonds
Or pacify the lions
But you know you can never make me
Love u more.
You can make me dance to order
My self hung, torn and quartered
But you know you can never make me
Love u more.

Let the new day hide
Leave the scars inside
Still you know you can never make me
Love u more.
Let the rain pour down
Let the valleys drown
Still you know you can never make me
Hey, you know you can never make me
Love u more.

Verse 3:
We can make the sun turn purple
We can make the sea turn turtle
But you know you can never make me
Love u more.
We can turn wine into water
Turn sadness into laughter
But you know you can never make me
Love u more.

Let the sky fall down
Let the leaves turn brown
Still you know you can never make me
Love u more.
Let the redwoods die
As the wells run dry
Still you know you can never make me
Yeah, you know you can never make me
Love u more.

STAY WITH ME

Words & Music by Craig Joiner, Anthony Mitman & Robert John 'Mutt' Lange

♩ = 80

1. When I close my eyes___ and you're not there,___ I feel this emp-ti-ness___ in-side,___ do you care?___ If you have to go___ I'll un-der-stand,___ but the pain's___

so hard to take when we're a - part. 2. You'll nev - er see me cry,

it's locked a - way but there's this feel-ing deep with-in me wants to stay.

(Verses 3 & 4 see block lyric)

And if you were here would things be right?

I need to find my way a - lone to win this fight.

Verse 3:

And there's just no point in looking back
And finding fault in everything we ever had
And the promises we made with tears
Will always be with me in times–when you're not here.

Stay with me *etc.*

Verse 4:

If I hold you close no need to fight
I know that nothing I could say would make it right
If the chance has gone, slipped away
Before you leave there's just one thing I've got to say.

Stay with me *etc.*